At Every Turn! It's Ballet

By STEPHANIE RIVA SORINE

Photographs by
DANIEL S. SORINE

Alfred A. Knopf
New York

This is a Borzoi Book
Published by Alfred A. Knopf, Inc.

Copyright © 1981 by Stephanie Riva Sorine and Daniel S. Sorine
All rights reserved under International and Pan-American Copyright Conventions.
Published in the United States by Alfred A. Knopf, Inc.,
New York, and simultaneously in Canada by Random House
of Canada Limited, Toronto.
Distributed by Random House, Inc., New York.
Library of Congress Cataloging in Publication Data
Sorine, Stephanie Riva.
At every turn! It's ballet.
Summary: Reveals how everyday movements such as
stretching, skipping, and jumping are
transformed into ballet.
1. Ballet—Juvenile literature.   [1. Ballet]
I. Sorine, Daniel S.   II. Title.
GV1787.5.S65   1981   792.8   80-20808
ISBN 0-394-84473-4 (Tr.)   ISBN 0-394-94473-9 (lib. bdg.)
Designed by Mina Greenstein
Manufactured in the United States of America
3   5   7   9   0   8   6   4   2

Very special thanks to our editor, Pat Ross, and to the others at Alfred A. Knopf who also contributed their expertise to the production of this book, including Andrea Brown, Linn Fischer and Mina Greenstein.

Big kisses and hugs and thanks to the children for their participation: Gregory Bayer, Lauren and Haley Fox, Tyler Ingram, Wendi Maguire and Erica Ross.

For everyone, everywhere…

Stephanie and Daniel Sorine

*We do ballet.
You can, too.*

A ballet dancer leaps and seems to touch the sky. Another dancer twirls and suddenly becomes a blur of color. Their bodies are light and strong and graceful. They move so swiftly, they seem to fly. Or so slowly, they seem frozen in space. They spin out a mood, an idea, a story. Through the motion of their bodies, they create such an exciting performance that you want to shout: "Bravo!"

As you watch dancers move across a stage in ways that seem incredible, you might think, "I could never do that!"

But every day, you use your body in much the same way that ballet dancers use theirs.

It starts with the way *you* move—at home, at school, in the playground. You stretch to reach a high shelf, spin around to catch a fast ball, skip down the street. Then you leap across a puddle and jump for joy that you made it without getting wet! Dancers reach, spin, skip, leap, and jump for joy, too.

It is no accident, though, when a dancer moves with tremendous power or balances perfectly, making each step look light and easy. Hours of daily exercise make a dancer's muscles strong and flexible. Years of practice develop coordination, skill, and style. Only then can the dancer change everyday movements into the different and beautiful language of ballet.

But remember: Ballet begins with you.

The ballet dancers in this book are Wendi Maguire and Tyler Ingram. Compare their movements to those of Gregory Bayer, Erica Ross, and Lauren and Haley Fox, who are not ballet dancers. In *At Every Turn! It's Ballet* you will see their everyday motions—and your own—turned into the language of dance.

Stephanie Riva Sorine

Ballet is everywhere, because...

Ballet uses everyday movements:

Reaching.

Squatting.

Bouncing and bounding.

Bending.

Crouching.

Kneeling.

And balancing.

Hold on now!

These are the ways you move, too.

You jump

across puddles.

You jump

from benches.

You jump

so high.

At every turn! It's ballet.

Remember, ballet begins with you.

It's what you do.

It's how you move.

Yoo-hoo!

turns into ballet.

Ballet changes the ways you move.

Stretch and reach.

Ballet...

It's helpful, too.

Oh! I can leap with power and grace.

What about me?

I can look as light as lace.

Can I?

I try!

Ballet is precise.

Ballet is special, and...

We do. You can, too!

Stephanie Riva Sorine grew up in Woodbury, Long Island. She trained at the School of American Ballet and London's Royal Ballet School, danced as a soloist with the Austrian Ballet, and apprenticed with the Harkness Ballet. She teaches classes in ballet and dance movement to children and adults in New York City.

Daniel S. Sorine was born in Paris, France and raised in Monaco. He attended Le Rosey and Institut Florimont in Switzerland and Lycée Français de New York. His photographs have appeared in *Life, Time, Newsweek, People, TV Guide, The New York Times, Dancemagazine, New West,* and in other publications in America and abroad.

The Sorines, who now live in New York City, have been married since 1977, and are the authors of *Imagine That! It's Modern Dance,* as well as the highly acclaimed adult book, *Dancershoes,* and Ballantine's ballet calendars.